Proverbs For Daily Living

Compiled by
John P. Beilenson

Design by Michel Design

PETER PAUPER PRESS, INC.

WHITE PLAINS · NEW YORK

PROVERBS FOR
DAILY LIVING

NATURE HAS given us two ears, two eyes, and but one tongue, so we should hear and see more than we speak.

THE BEST physicians are Dr. Diet, Dr. Quiet, and Dr. Merryman.

THREE MAY keep a secret, if two of them are dead.

WHO MARRIES for love without money has good nights and sorry days.

IF YOU would reap praise,
you must sow the seeds:
gentle words and useful
deeds.

LOVE YOUR neighbor, but
don't pull down your hedge.

HOPE FOR the best, get ready for the worst, and then take what God chooses to send.

PATIENCE IS a tree whose root is bitter, but whose fruit is very sweet.

FORTUNE LOST, nothing lost; courage lost, much lost; honor lost, more lost; soul lost, all lost.

A BLIND person will not thank you for a looking glass.

THE HIGHER the ape goes,
the more he shows his tail.

A GOOD example is the best
sermon.

PROPHETS ARE without honor in their own countries, among their own kin and in their own houses.

BE AT war with your vices, at peace with your neighbors, and let every new month find you a better person.

PEOPLE WHO plant trees
love others besides
themselves.

GLASS, CHINA, and reputation
are easily cracked and never
well mended.

IF SOMEONE works for you,
you work for them.

THE OPPOSITE side has its
opposite side.

SAY WELL and do well end
with one letter. Say well is
good, but do well is better.

BOOKS ARE the masters who
instruct us without hard
words or anger, food or pay.

ANGER AND folly walk side by side; repentance treads on both their heels.

A FAULT once denied is twice committed.

IF YOU wish to know the
character of the prince, look
at his ministers. If you wish to
understand the person, look
at his or her friends. If you
wish to know the parent,
look at the child.

A GEM is not polished without rubbing, nor a person perfected without trials.

CAST NO dirt into the well that gives you water.

GOD COMES at last when we think the Almighty is farthest off.

THE WAY to Hell is paved with good intentions, the way to Heaven with good works.

BETTER TO be alone than in bad company.

PEOPLE WHO listen to what others say of them will never have peace.

THERE IS nothing so eloquent as a rattlesnake's tail.

SEARCH OTHERS for their virtues, yourself for your vices.

FAULTS ARE thick where love
is thin.

A FALSE friend and a shadow
attend only while the sun
shines.

DON'T PRAY when it's raining, if you don't pray when the sun is shining.

YOU HAVE the rest of your life to figure out what to do with the rest of your life.

A THREEFOLD cord is not quickly broken.

A LIVING dog is better than a dead lion.

AN OPEN rebuke is better than secret love.

A SHIP in harbour is safe, but that is not what ships are built for.

WILLIAM SHEDD

IF THE dogs are barking at your heels, you know you're leading the pack.

TWO VOICES cannot be perceived in one ear.

TALMUD

THE LENDER is greater than
he who performs charity; but
he who forms a partnership
with the poor is greater than
all.

TALMUD

WHERE THE needle goes,
the thread follows.

YOU VOTE with your life.

WHAT'S THE use of running when you're not on the right road.

WHERE THE bees are, there is honey.

YOU WILL not go to heaven if not content to go alone.

THE POOR have little, beggars
none; the rich too much,
enough not one.

THERE IS no better looking
glass than an old friend.

IF YOU think twice before you speak once, you will speak better for it.

WHEN THE lamps in the house are lighted, it is like the flowering of the lotus on the lake.

A GOOD friend speaks well of us behind our backs.

NEITHER SPEAK well nor ill of yourself. If well, people will not believe you; if ill, they will believe a great deal more than you say.

TO ENJOY a lifetime
romance—fall in love
with yourself.

IF YOU'D have a servant that
you like, serve yourself.

WORDS MAY show a person's wit, but action a person's meaning.

SOLOMON MADE a book of proverbs, but a book of proverbs never made a Solomon.

IF YOU take fire into your
heart, your clothes are likely
to burn.

HATRED STIRS up strife; love
covers all sins.

HOPE DEFERRED makes the
heart sick.

A SOFT answer turns away
anger.

BEFORE HONOR is humility.

IRON SHARPENS iron, so a
person sharpens the intellect
of a friend.

TEACH YOUR tongue to say,
"I do not know," lest you err
and stumble through your
error.

TALMUD

WHEN THE mouse is full, the
bread tastes stale.

GIVE THE nut to the beauty,
and the rose to the safe.

ON A dangerous road, wear
your beard over your shoulder.

THE BIRD is small, but the
beak is sharp.

ONE DOG barks at his
shadow. A hundred bark at
his sound.

WISE BEES don't sip from
fallen flowers.

THE DOOR to virtue is heavy
and hard to push.

ENOUGH SHOVELS of earth—
a mountain.

ENOUGH PAILS of water—a
river.

DO NOT pray for gold. Pray for good children and happy grandchildren.

WHEN THE mantis hunts the locust, he forgets the shrike that's hunting him.

LEARNING IS like rowing
upstream. Advance or lose all.

LONG ROADS test the horse;
long dealings the friend.

WHO FAILS to eat is undone;
who fails a business is
undone; who fails in court is
undone; who fails with his or
her mother-in-law is undone.

DIVIDE AN orange. It tastes
just as good.

A DROP of water falling on a red-hot iron vanishes without leaving a trace. The same drop falling on a lotus-leaf shines like a pearl. The same drop falling into an oyster becomes a pearl. Thus people who associate with the inferior, the ordinary, and the superior respond accordingly.

ENTERTAINMENT BRINGS
relatives, and flattery brings
fortune.

FALL FROM a house and you
may be saved; fall from public
respect and you are lost.

SLOW WORK is fine work.

MEDITATION SHOULD be done alone; study by two together; musical practice by three; traveling by four; agriculture by five; and battle by many.

A BAD word whispered will echo a hundred miles.

STICK TO one thing and all will come; aim at everything and all will go.

IF THE first words fail, ten
thousand will not then avail.

FREE YOUR mind and the
rest will follow.

TEACHERS OPEN the door,
but you enter by yourself.

THE LIGHT of a thousand
stars does not make one
moon.

WHERE THERE are many
hands, the lentils get burned.

HE WHOM a serpent has
stung is afraid of the rope.

DO NOT shoot arrows at an iron statue.

NEW THINGS are the best things; old friends are the best friends.

THE BEGINNING of learning
is silence, then comes hear-
ing, then writing, then work,
then promulgation.

SPEECH IS a beautiful net in
which souls are caught.

IF THY trouble is in good works, know the trouble will pass and the good works remain; if thy pleasure is in sin, know the pleasure will pass and the sin remain.

SILENCE IS the sibling of assent.

IN A quarrel between bulls,
it's the calf's leg that gets
broken.

IF IT is given with love, a
mere handful is enough.

A MEAN man promises and does not; a good man promises but does.

A GOOD man says no slowly; a wise man says no at once.

THE CHURCH is near, but the road is all ice; the tavern is far, but I'll walk very carefully.

YOU CAN'T sip soup with a knife.

WHERE WISDOM is perfect,
words are few.

WHEN TWO dogs fight, let
the third keep his distance.

THE PRINCE of a people is its servant.

THE INGENIOUS man without morals is like the strong man without weapons.

OPEN YOUR umbrella before
you get wet.

IF YOU make yourself a dog,
make yourself a rich man's
dog.

LUCKY IS having a rice
dumpling fly into your mouth.

EVEN THE prettiest shoe
makes a sorry hat.

BIG TREES provoke the pride
of the winds.

DON'T JUDGE the tree till
you see the fruit.

BETTER COVER the fish than chase the cat.

THE COUPLE'S quarrel and the west wind die down at dark.

SPARROWS KNOW not the dreams of swans.

TO LIVE long: keep a cool head and warm feet.

TO UNDERSTAND a parent's
love: have a child.

CAREFUL HOW you handle
scissors and fools.

MOTHER IS always right.

THE TALLEST trees are often leveled by the storm.

NOT THE lover, but his language wins the lady.

DON'T USE the ox-cleaver to kill a hen.

WHO SITS in the shade won't take an axe to the tree.

TO TEACH is also to learn.